USING THIS BOOK

*One of the best ways of helping children to learn to read is by reading stories to them and with them. This way they learn what **reading** is, and they will gradually come to recognise many words, and begin to read for themselves.*

First, grown-ups read the story on the left-hand pages aloud to the child.

You can reread the story as often as the child enjoys hearing it. Talk about the pictures as you go.

Later the child is encouraged to read the words under the pictures on the right-hand page.

The pages at the back of the book will give you some ideas for helping your child to read.

British Library Cataloguing in Publication Data
McCullagh, Sheila K.
　The monster loses his beard. — (Puddle Lane. Stage 1; 18).
　1. Readers —1950-
　I. Title　　II. Morris, Tony, *1938 Aug. 2-*　　III. Series
　428.6　　PE1119
　ISBN 0-7214-1019-7

First edition

Published by Ladybird Books Ltd Loughborough Leicestershire UK
Ladybird Books Inc Lewiston Maine 04240 USA

The monster loses his beard

written by SHEILA McCULLAGH
illustrated by TONY MORRIS

This book belongs to:

Ladybird Books

Tim and Tessa Catchamouse
woke up early one morning.
Their mother, Pegs,
was just coming in
through the hole that led
to the garden.
"I'm hungry," said Tim.
"So am I," said Tessa.

Tim and Tessa
woke up.

"It's time you learnt to catch fish,"
said Pegs. "Come with me,
and I'll show you what to do."
They all went into the garden.
They hadn't gone far,
when Pegs suddenly said, "Hide!"
They hid in the long grass.

"Hide!" said Pegs.

"What is it?" whispered Tessa.
"Sh!" said Pegs.
"There's a monster in the garden.
He's very gruff and grumpy,
and he puffs out fire and smoke.
He'll chase you, if he sees you."

"Sh!" said Pegs.

Tim and Tessa could hear
someone huffing and puffing.
They looked out between some stones.
The monster was standing
under a tree,
not very far away.

The monster was
under a tree.

As they watched, the monster vanished.

"He's gone," said Tim.

"No, he hasn't," said Pegs.

"You can still see his ears."

They waited, until

the two red ears disappeared.

"Come on," said Pegs.

"We can go now."

The monster vanished.

They came to a big lake.
"This way," said Pegs.
They went along the lake,
till they came to a stream.

the big lake

They followed the stream
to the wall of the garden.
"This way," said Pegs.
She ran up a tree,
on to the wall.
Tim and Tessa followed her.

Pegs ran up a tree.

Pegs jumped down
on the other side, and
Tim and Tessa jumped after her.
They found themselves
on the bank of the stream.
"This is a good place to fish,"
said Pegs. "Watch."
She crouched down
on the bank of the stream,
and looked down.

Pegs looked down.

Suddenly, Pegs jumped
into the water.
She went right under, and
came up with a fish
in her mouth.
She jumped up on to the bank.

Pegs jumped up.

Tim and Tessa ate the fish.

"Now you catch one," said Pegs.

Tim looked back.

"I don't like getting wet," he said.

"If you don't get wet,
you'll never catch fish," said Pegs.

Tessa looked into the water.

Tim looked back.
Tessa looked down.

A fish swam by.
Tessa jumped in.
The water went into her eyes
and into her ears.
It went into her mouth, too.
She came out spluttering, and
splashed her way up the bank.
"I couldn't see anything," she said.

Tessa came out.

"You have to practise," said Pegs.
Tim looked at Tessa.
She was very wet.
"I'll do better than that,"
he said.
He saw a fish, and jumped in.

Tim jumped in.

A minute later,
Tim splashed his way up the bank.
"It got away," he said, gasping.
"You'll learn how to do it,
if you try hard," said Pegs.

"It got away,"
said Tim.

Tim and Tessa tried all morning,
and in the end
they each caught a little fish.
Pegs caught a big one.
"We'll go home now,
and get dry," she said.

"We will go home,"
said Pegs.

They had just got to the lake,
when they heard a great roar,
and there was the monster!
Tim and Tessa hid.
The monster didn't like cats,
but he did like fish for supper.
"Give me that fish!" he roared.
Pegs looked at the monster.
She put down the fish.
"This is our supper, not yours,"
she said.

Pegs looked
at the monster.

The monster roared in fury.
Fire and smoke
shot out of his mouth.
But at that moment,
a gust of wind
blew the monster's beard sideways,
and the beard was caught in the flames.
The monster's beard was on fire!

The monster's beard
was on fire!

The monster gave another roar,
but it was a roar of fright.
He jumped into the lake,
and disappeared under the water.

The monster jumped
into the lake.

"Quick!" cried Pegs. "Run!"
She picked up the fish,
and the three cats ran back
to their home under the steps
as fast as they could run.

The cats ran home.

They had just finished supper,
when they heard
a snuffling sound outside.
Tim and Tessa looked out.
The monster was in the garden.
He was getting dry
by a fire.
He looked very miserable.
"He's lost his beard," said Tessa.
"He shouldn't blow fire at cats,"
said Tim. "He'll know that, another time."

The monster was
in the garden.

Notes for the parent/teacher

When you have read the story, go back to the beginning. Look at each picture and talk about it, pointing to the caption below, and reading it aloud yourself.

Run your finger along under the words as you read, so that the child learns that reading goes from left to right. (You needn't say this in so many words. Children learn many useful things about reading by just reading with you, and it is often better to let them learn by experience, rather than by explanation.) When you next go through the book, encourage the child to read the words and sentences under the illustrations.

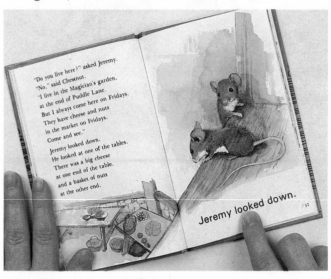

Jeremy looked down.

Don't rush in with the word before he* has time to think, but don't leave him struggling for too long. Always encourage him to feel that he is reading successfully, praising him when he does well, and avoiding criticism.

Now turn back to the beginning, and print the child's name in the space on the title page, using ordinary, not capital letters. Let him watch you print it: this is another useful experience.

*Children enjoy hearing the same story many times. Read this one as often as the child likes hearing it. The more opportunities he has of looking at the illustrations and **reading** the captions with you, the more he will come to recognise the words. Don't worry if he **remembers** rather than **reads** the captions. This is a normal stage in learning.*

If you have a number of books, let him choose which story he would like to have again.

---

*Footnote: In order to avoid the continual "he or she", "him or her", the child is referred to in this book as "he". However, the stories are equally appropriate for girls and boys.

43

*There are more stories about another monster
called the Griffle in these books:*

Stage 1

the Griffle

Stage 2

*Here is another story
about the Gruffle:*

Stage 3

*from
The Gruffle
in Puddle Lane*